Building Faces: Identities Restored

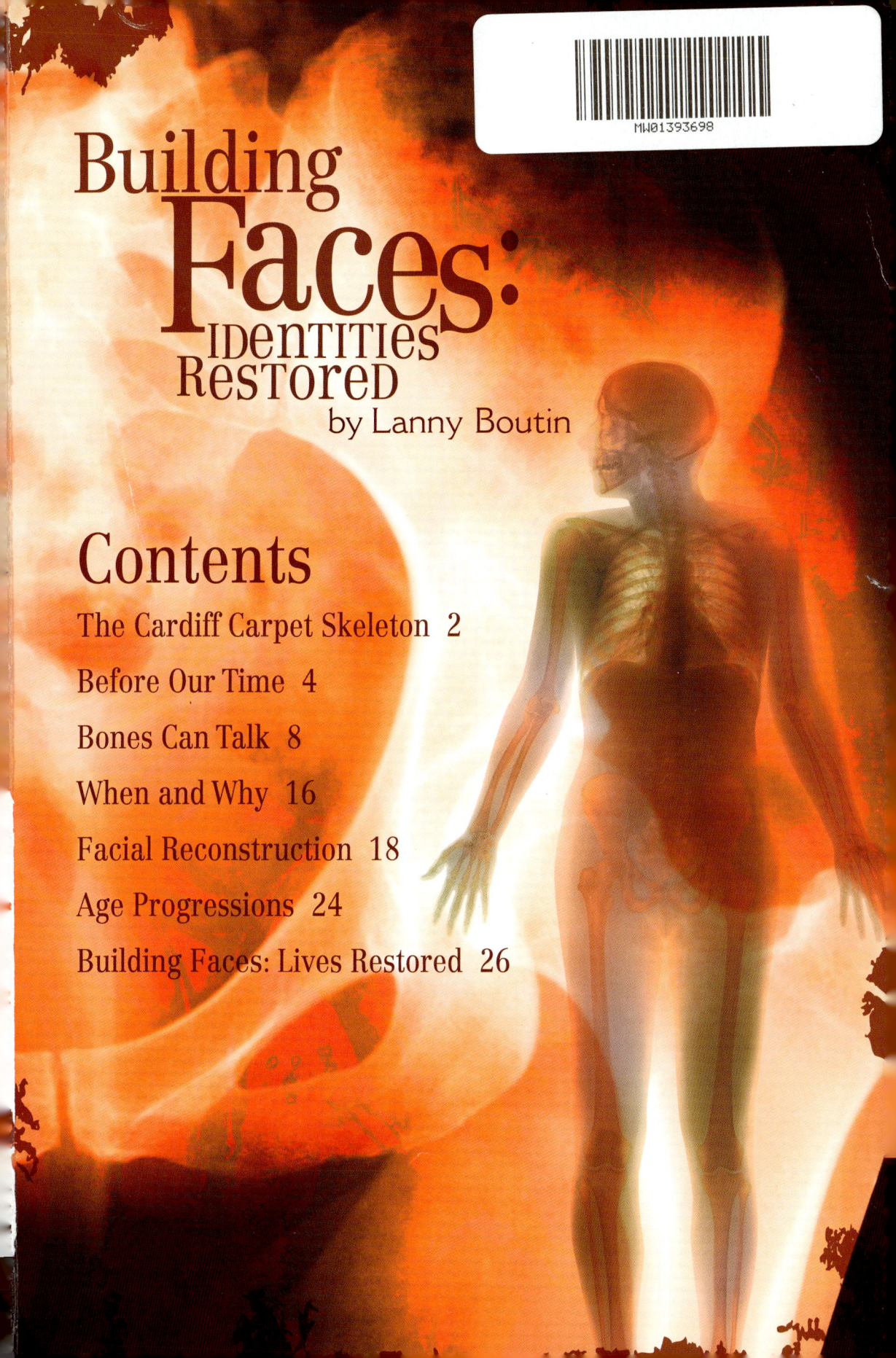

by Lanny Boutin

Contents

The Cardiff Carpet Skeleton 2

Before Our Time 4

Bones Can Talk 8

When and Why 16

Facial Reconstruction 18

Age Progressions 24

Building Faces: Lives Restored 26

The Cardiff Carpet Skeleton

On a cold December day in 1989, in Cardiff, Wales, construction workers stumbled upon a grisly find. While laying drainpipes in the backyard of an abandoned house, they discovered a rolled carpet buried just below the ground. Wrapped up in that carpet were bones. Human bones.

It was obvious the bones had been there for some time. Police scoured the area for evidence, but there was little to go on. A professor from the local dental school examined the skeleton's teeth. He was able to estimate the age of the deceased. Police checked their missing persons files but came up with nothing.

Who was this mystery person wrapped in a carpet, and how had he or she gotten there? Finally, with no leads to follow, investigators decided to ask a forensic artist to recreate the skeleton's face in hopes of restoring its identity.

CLOSE READING

Explain the author's technique for introducing the topic of facial reconstruction.

Wrapped up in that carpet were bones

Before Our Time

More than 8,000 years ago, the people of Jericho, in the Jordan Valley, practiced facial reconstruction. Under the floor of one of their homes, an archaeologist found nine human skulls. Each had been carefully covered with numerous layers of clay, realistically depicting the original facial features it had supported. Seashells were embedded into the clay for eyes. Other similar skulls have been found in the area over the years.

In the early 1800s, European scientists started toying with the idea of reconstructing faces. They used crude tools such as pins and sewing needles to measure the thickness of the skin and muscle in the faces of cadavers. They also began cataloguing the sizes and shapes of skulls.

In 1895, in one of the first truly scientific uses of facial reconstruction, Professor Wilhelm His, a German anatomist (a person who studies the human body), set out to see whether the bones found in a grave in Leipzig, Germany, really were those of composer Johann Sebastian Bach (1685-1750). His's reconstruction turned out to bear an amazing likeness to contemporary portraits of Bach. That removed any doubt that the bones were truly Bach's. Over the next few years, other scientists followed His's lead, recreating the faces of other famous people.

FIRST READING

How old is the science of facial reconstruction?

That removed any doubt that the bones were truly Bach's

Another experiment in the early 1900s didn't work out as well. Scientist Von Eggeling, also from Germany, decided to pit two artists against each other by asking them both to do a facial reconstruction of the same skull.

First, a cast (or mask) was made of the dead man's face, to show what he really looked like. Then, two exact copies of the skull were made. Each artist was given one and asked to reconstruct the face.

When they had finished, Von Eggeling discovered, to his astonishment, that the two recreations looked totally different. Worse yet, neither looked at all like the dead man!

The scientific community was shaken. The whole process of facial reconstruction ground to a halt. For years it was left to the realm of detective fiction.

Scientists don't discourage easily, however. By the late 1960s, scientists in the United States, USSR, and Britain were again quietly working to perfect the process.

FIRST READING
Which of the artist's recreations looked like the dead man?

In the 1970s, another experiment was performed. This one was arranged like a police line-up. With the help of the U.S. Federal Aviation Authority, anthropologists circulated photos of two completed facial reconstructions—one of a man and one of a woman—along with photos of them before they died and photos of a handful of other people.

The pictures were shown to both police officers and ordinary citizens to see if they could match the reconstruction with the correct photo. Two-thirds of those shown the photos were able to match the photo of the man to his reconstruction correctly. With the woman, whose photo was 25 years old, only a quarter managed to get it right. The results, however, were still good enough to make people believe that reliable facial reconstructions were possible.

Scientists still refer to facial reconstruction as an approximate science. Unlike a photo, it only gives investigators a likeness of the person—a likeness that they hope will trigger some sort of useful recognition.

> **CLOSE READING**
> What is the most important idea in paragraph 2 above?

Male pelvis

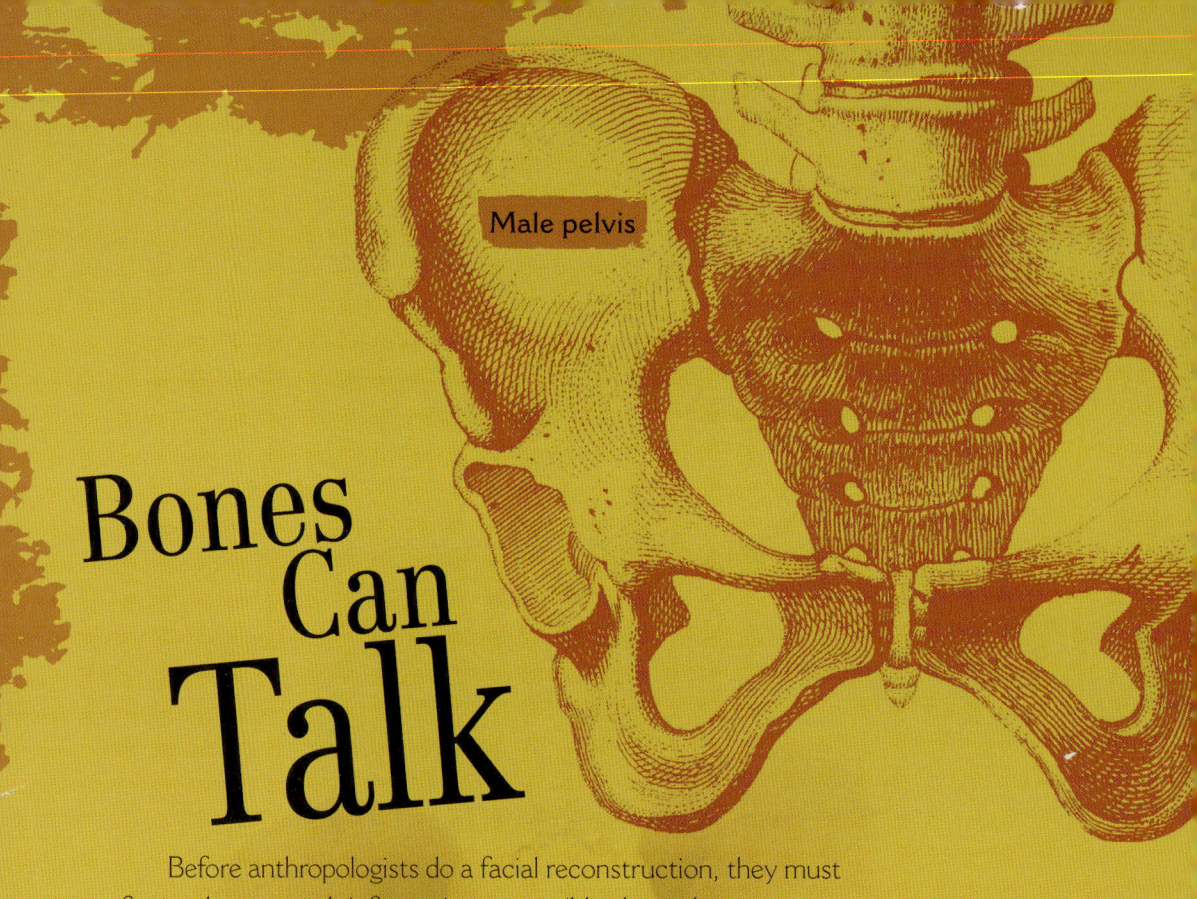

Bones Can Talk

Before anthropologists do a facial reconstruction, they must first gather as much information as possible about the person.

This is done by looking at the artifacts found with the body. Watches, jewelry, and even hair accessories found with the body can suggest whether the skeleton is that of a woman or a man. Bits of clothing can give hints to the person's age or nationality, even their occupation.

Sometimes investigators are lucky. They find concrete clues that tell them who the person was, but often there is nothing left behind for them to study except bones.

Bones do talk. To the trained eye, they can deliver a lot of useful information about who the person was and how they got there. Scientists today typically use two different methods to read bones. First they observe, then they measure.

First they observe, then they me

Female pelvis

The Big Four—Gender

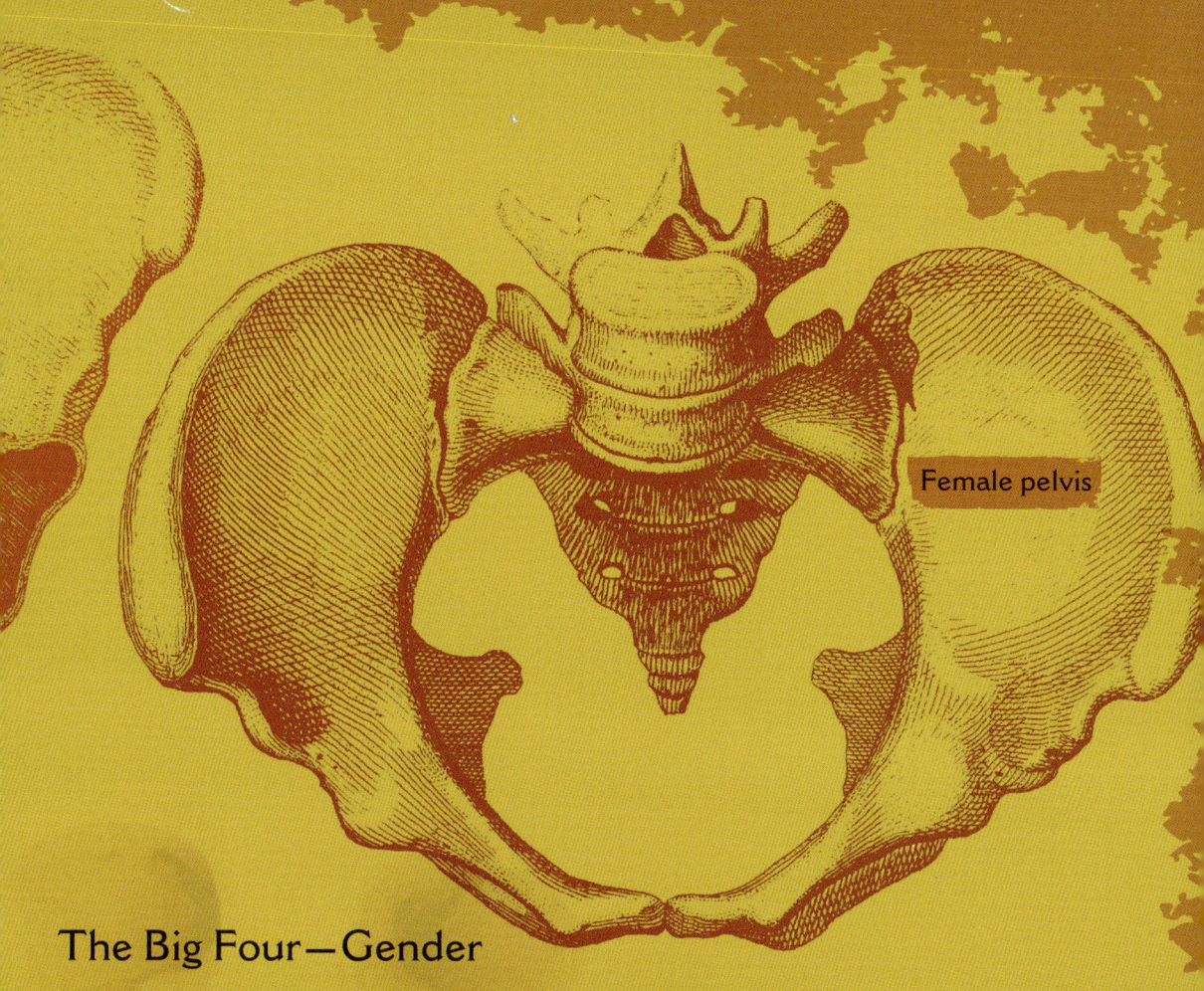

The first thing to be established is the person's gender. It can be determined in a few different ways. Forensic archaeologists measure the size of the skeleton. Research shows that the men in any group are typically larger than the women.

Size is often relatively useless without knowing the age and the nationality of the person. A better way to determine the gender of a skeleton is by measuring the height and width of the pelvic bones. A woman's pelvic bones are typically shorter and wider than a man's. This is to allow space for childbirth.

A man's skull is also generally wider and taller than a woman's skull. A woman's skull is usually smoother, with fewer ridges than a man's.

CLOSE READING

Why does the author say that size is useless without knowing the age or nationality?

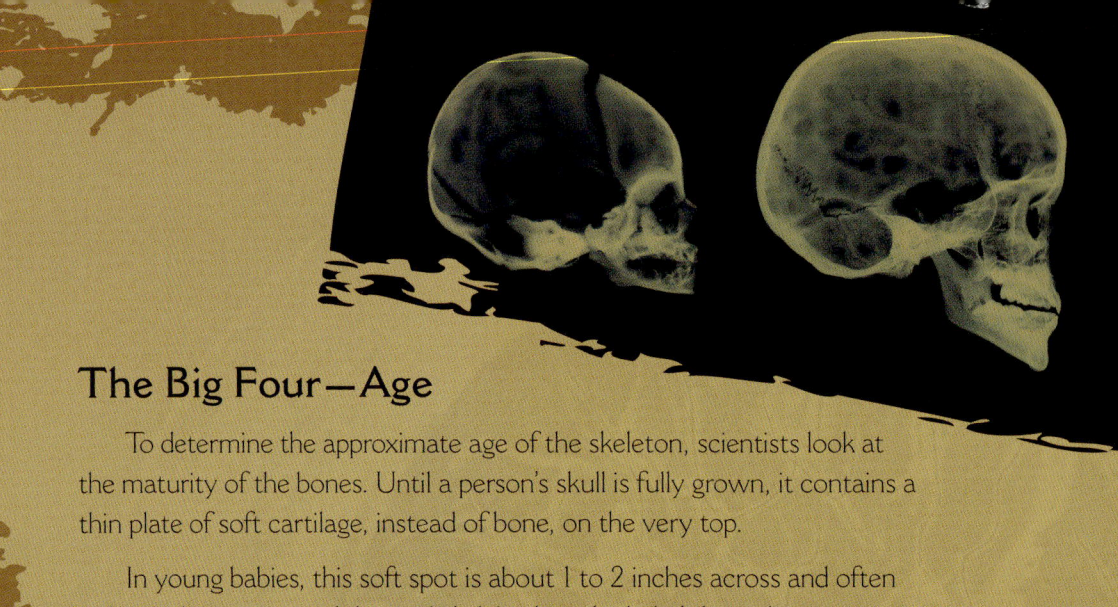

The Big Four—Age

To determine the approximate age of the skeleton, scientists look at the maturity of the bones. Until a person's skull is fully grown, it contains a thin plate of soft cartilage, instead of bone, on the very top.

In young babies, this soft spot is about 1 to 2 inches across and often pulsates (moves up and down slightly) when the baby's heart beats.

As a baby ages, the skull bones grow together, and the soft spot disappears. It is usually completely gone by the time the baby is about 15 months old. A skull from someone in the 18 to 23-year-old range still shows rough suture lines where the skull grew together. By the time a person is in their 60s, these lines have all but faded.

The long bones in the body—the bones of the arms and legs—don't fuse to their cartilage caps at the joints until after the age of 20. As we age, our bones also become less dense and more porous. They start to wear down, and lower back problems become more noticeable. Again, this is only an approximate guide.

A person's occupation, health, and exercise patterns play a large role in how quickly their bones age. Regular exercise contributes to healthy muscles, which in turn help to shield bones from damage.

If they are intact, the teeth, like those of our Cardiff Carpet Skeleton, can also reveal age. We typically get our baby teeth between the ages of 6 months and 30 months. Depending on the type of tooth, our adult teeth emerge between the ages of 6 years and 21 years. Determining age by looking at the teeth is much harder in adult skeletons, but it can be done.

FIRST READING

What is the approximate length of time that any evidence of a soft spot exists?

As we age, tooth loss increases and the amount of bone in our jaw decreases. Archaeologists also look at tooth wear and the color of the teeth. Teeth tend to yellow with age.

Again, these tests aren't foolproof. People lose teeth for many reasons: accidents, poor hygiene, and even cosmetic reasons. Similarly, teeth change color at different rates, depending on the food we eat and the medications we take. Some sugary drinks wear down the teeth's outer enamel, making them appear older. Even stress can make your teeth age faster.

So some anthropologists are now counting the rings of cementum—a bone-like material—around a tooth's roots to determine age. Just like a tree, which adds a new ring to its trunk each year, the human tooth adds a ring of cementum around its root. Why this happens is not known. However, by taking a thin slice of a tooth's root and analyzing it under a powerful microscope, a scientist can count the number of rings and get a pretty good idea of the person's age.

FIRST READING

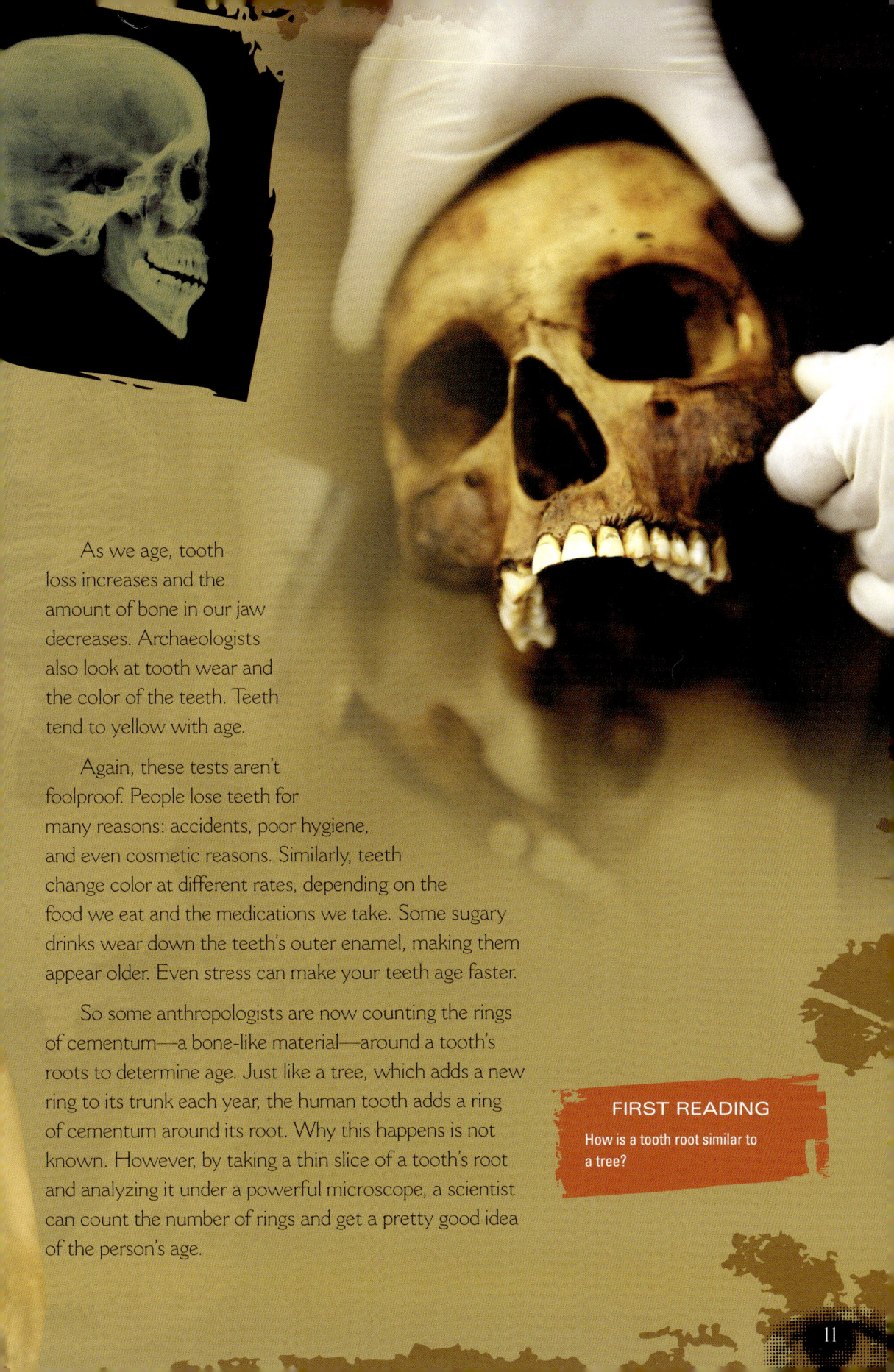

How is a tooth root similar to a tree?

The Big Four—Nationality

Nationality is also extremely important in determining facial features and identity. Again, it must be guessed at, using observation and measurements. Racial differences, such as high foreheads and other distinctive bone structures, can easily be confused with differences in gender or age. The often-smaller stature of a person of Asian descent can easily be confused with the smaller stature of a Caucasian youth. Anthropologists must look at many different clues.

Even the hole left in the skull where the nose was can be used to help establish identity. The hole is typically round in Native Americans and long and narrow in the Caucasian population. The skull of a person of African descent is usually low and narrow, compared to the typically-higher and wider Caucasian skull. How far the upper and lower jaws stick out can also be a strong indicator of ethnicity and nationality.

Teeth can also be studied to determine ethnicity. The incisors, or front teeth, are shaped like the blade of a knife in some nationalities. They appear more like a rounded shovel in others.

FIRST READING

According to the text, what factors have contributed to the difficulty of verifying nationality?

CLOSE READING

What inferences can you make about why there are differences in the shapes of teeth?

    Nationality gives the anthropologist important clues to a person's eye and hair color. Eye color is determined by the type of pigment in the iris of the eye, and even the slightest change in eye color can make a big difference in the way a person looks. Brown is the dominant eye color in the world. People with blue eyes make up around eight percent of the world's population. Only about five percent of the world's population have green eyes.

    Verifying nationality is becoming increasingly difficult. Since the end of the last world war, the increase in immigration to this country has been phenomenal. Interracial marriages are also becoming more common, and the lines between nationalities are rapidly blurring.

to ethnicity

The Big Four—Stature

The size of a person is also very important in determining his or her identity. Using formulas created over the years, such as measurements of the femur, the long bone in the thigh, or the tibia, the larger of the two bones in the calf, scientists can now quite accurately determine how tall a person was without having an entire skeleton.

The width of certain bones can also show how muscular a person was. Bone growth in the upper body is significantly affected by the growth of muscles and can tell scientists how much upper body strength a person might have had. The amount of wear and tear on the bones and joints also provides clues to how much a person weighed.

Bones provide other interesting clues. By looking at the marks on the bones where the muscles were attached to the wrist, you can even tell whether the person was left or right-handed.

Taken alone, none of these things—gender, age, nationality, or stature—can necessarily tell a scientist exactly who the person was. Together they help to build a picture of what he or she might have looked like. In the case of the Cardiff Carpet Skeleton, scientists were able to determine that she was female. They were also able to work out her approximate height, age, and even her hair color.

By looking at the marks
tell whether the person

FIRST READING

What are some things scientists can determine by measuring a person's bones?

n the bones... you can even was left or right-handed

When and Why

Anthropologists use many methods, including carbon dating of bones and the study of bugs found by the skeleton, to determine approximately when the person died. Time of death is extremely important. It not only helps the police to narrow down their list of missing persons, it also helps the artist doing the reconstruction with time-sensitive details, such as hairstyles. The Cardiff Carpet Skeleton, it was determined, had been wrapped up in the carpet for about nine years.

Anthropologists also check the skeleton very carefully for any damage. Antemortem injuries (those received before death) can sometimes be matched to X-rays of missing people. Different diseases leave their marks on the bones, giving scientists clues to the person's health. Lines visible on the teeth, for example, can indicate a person who took a certain antibiotic at a particular time in their life. Particular kinds of injury to the fingers might suggest that the person had a job that involved heavy lifting or manual labor.

FIRST READING
What can time of death help scientists determine?

Anthropologists also look for injuries inflicted at the time of death, including indentations (cuts or nicks) in the bone, which could prove that the person did not die naturally. Postmortem injuries (injuries received after death) can also point to foul play. Even if the Cardiff Carpet Skeleton had died of natural causes, it's unlikely she could have rolled herself up in a carpet in a shallow grave without someone else's intervention.

CLOSE READING

How can indentions in the bone help prove that a person did not die naturally?

Time of death is extremely important...

17

Facial Reconstruction

3-D

When police officers delivered a copy of the Cardiff Carpet Skeleton's skull to the artist for reconstruction, it would have been placed on a special viewing stand that allows the artist to work on it from all angles. Using information on skin and muscle depths, or tissue depths, collected over the years, the artist then fastens tissue markers, or pegs, to the skull. These markers, which are often cut from thin wood about the size of a pencil eraser, help to guide the artist. There are usually between 15 and 34 markers, each cut to the appropriate length and then glued to specific spots around the skull. This soon gives the skull a porcupine look.

Once all the pegs are in place, the process of slowly rebuilding the face begins. The modeling material—usually clay, but sometimes wax or paste—is cut into flat, thin strips. These strips are then slowly laid over the skull, layer by layer, until the proper thickness at each part of the skull is reached. This is a very slow and exact process. Once all the strips are added, the clay is smoothed to remove any seams between the sections. Again, this must be done very carefully, taking care not to indent the clay or change its depth.

The nose is rebuilt by following the shape of the bone at the top of the nose hole down and the bone on the bottom of the hole outwards. The width of the nose is determined by the width of the hole. The hole is typically three-fifths of the width of the finished nose. The width of the mouth is established by measuring the distance between the skull's canine teeth.

> **FIRST READING**
> How many tissue markers are usually used in facial reconstruction?

Using the information from the skeleton, glass eyes in the proper color for the person's nationality are fitted into the skull. Other features, such as eyebrows, eyelids, and the line of the lips, are carefully added or molded into the clay, giving the reconstruction an eerily human look. Hair is also added, either in clay or using a wig. False teeth are used if they are needed.

The forensic artists worked almost around the clock on the three-dimensional (3-D) reconstruction of the Cardiff Carpet Skeleton, completing it in only two days. The reconstructed skull was then featured on a TV show about crime investigations.

Within 10 days of the show's airing, the Cardiff Carpet Skeleton was identified, by two different people from two different parts of Britain, as 15-year-old local girl Karen Price. Karen had disappeared in 1981, almost 9 years earlier. Dental records and DNA tests were able to confirm her identity and, with her identity known, her killers were soon brought to justice.

CLOSE READING

Reread the second paragraph on page 18. Does the author present the information effectively? Why or why not?

2-D

Three-dimensional reconstructions are the most advanced reconstruction treatments. However, because of limited finances or time restraints, often two-dimensional (2-D) facial reconstructions are done instead. Two-dimensional reconstructions start out similar to 3-D reconstructions, with tissue markers attached to the skull. Then an outline of the skull is drawn freehand. Or, more often now, it is captured through photography.

Using the tissue markers as a guide, the skull is carefully photographed from the side and the front. The photos are blown up to create a picture that is exactly the same size as the original skull. The photos are then securely attached to a hard surface and the skull's silhouette, or outline, is traced onto a transparent sheet. Now an artist can follow the outline of the skull and the tissue markers to draw a detailed likeness of the person.

Computers

One of the greatest additions to facial reconstruction techniques in recent years has been the computer. Hand-drawn or hand-sculpted reconstructions are slow and must be produced by experts with a lot of education and skill. They also create only one likeness of the person. Using specially designed computer software programs, forensic artists can now work faster and make multiple reconstructions that show many different facial options. Using a photograph or an X-ray of the skull, the facial reconstruction program allows the artists to manipulate any facial feature easily. They can make the ears smaller,

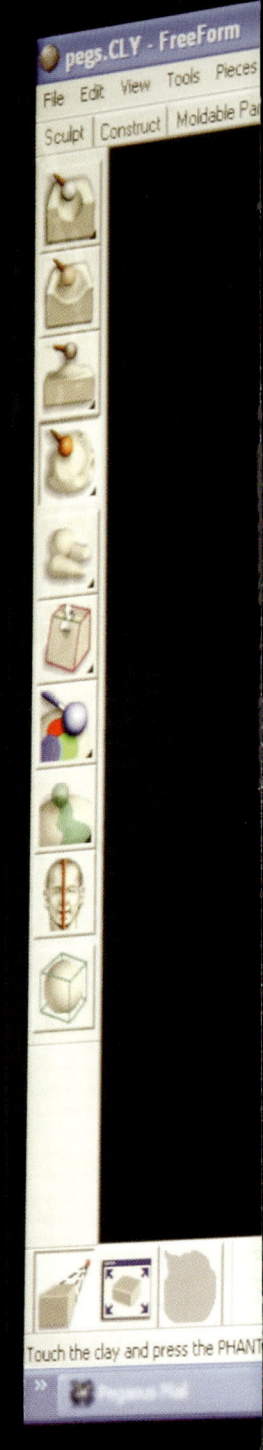

FIRST READING

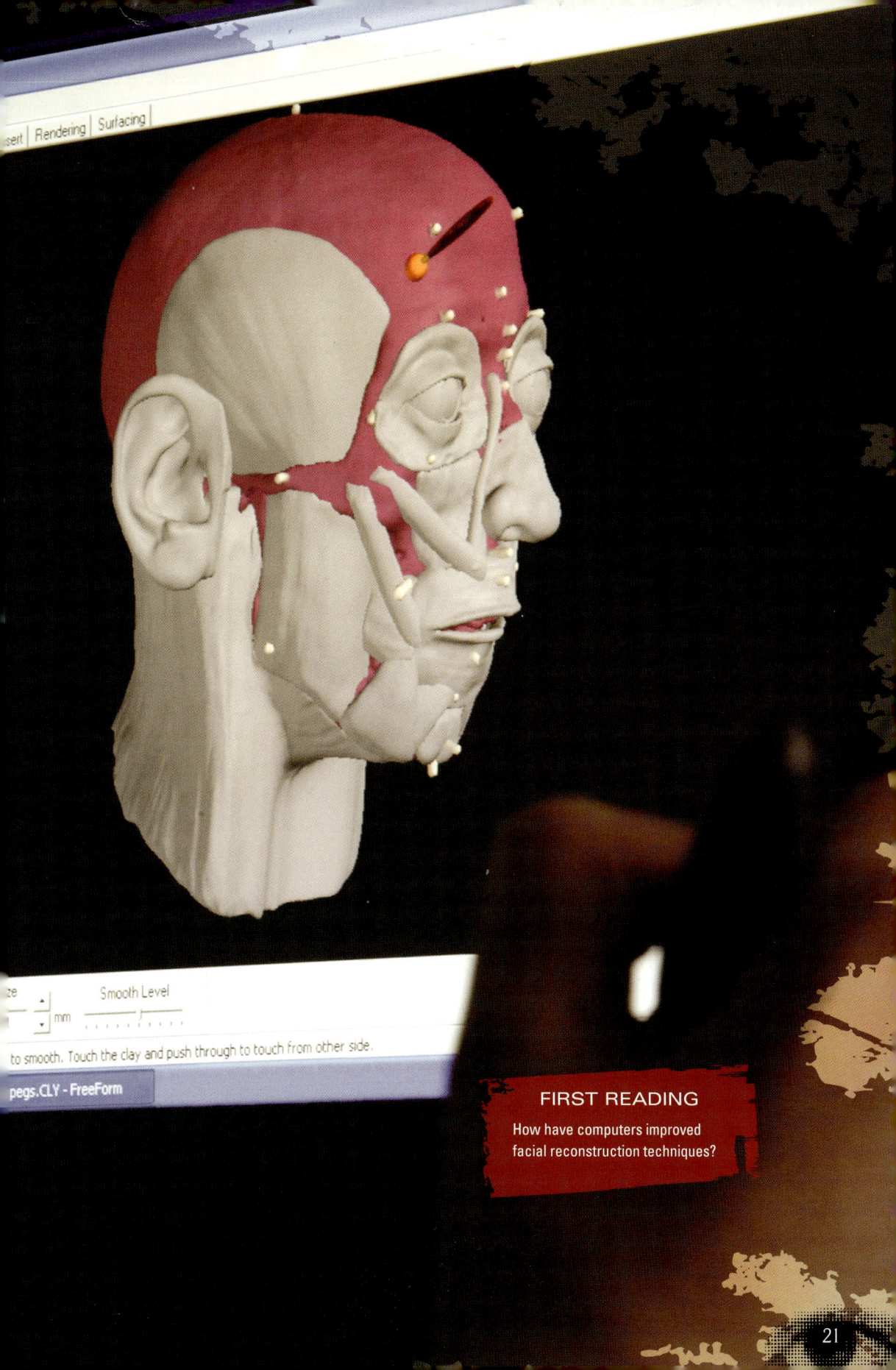

How have computers improved facial reconstruction techniques?

CT Scans

Sometimes scientists want to do a facial reconstruction on a skull that they are not allowed to touch. It is also possible that they cannot even see the skull, as was the case in the reconstruction of the Egyptian King Tutankhamun's face. Because King Tut is now a mummy, his skull is completely covered by mummified skin, so the scientists opted for a non-damaging computer tomography scan, or CT scan, to analyze the shape of King Tut's skull.

A CT scan is a special X-ray that takes hundreds of pictures similar to little slices through the body, creating an extremely detailed X-ray picture.

King Tut's mummy wasn't even removed from the tray of sand in which Howard Carter, the explorer who first found him, had placed him many years ago.

In January of 2005, the king's mummy was carefully moved from his tomb in the Valley of the Kings in Egypt to a nearby trailer containing a mobile CT scanner. During the next 15 minutes, some 1,700 images of the king were taken.

Not only did the CT scan give scientists a starting point to use for their reconstruction of the young king's face, it also answered some intriguing questions, such as how he died. The researchers who originally examined Tut's body concluded that the king, who died in 1,323 B.C.E. at the age of 18, was murdered. They believed that the damage visible on his skull proved that he must have died from a blow to the head. However, the CT scan showed that the damage was probably done long after the king's death, possibly in 1922, by Carter or one of his men. It also showed that the king's left leg had been badly fractured not long before his death. This, they guessed, could have contributed to his death.

FIRST READING
How did the CT scan help scientists discover more about how King Tut died?

CLOSE READING

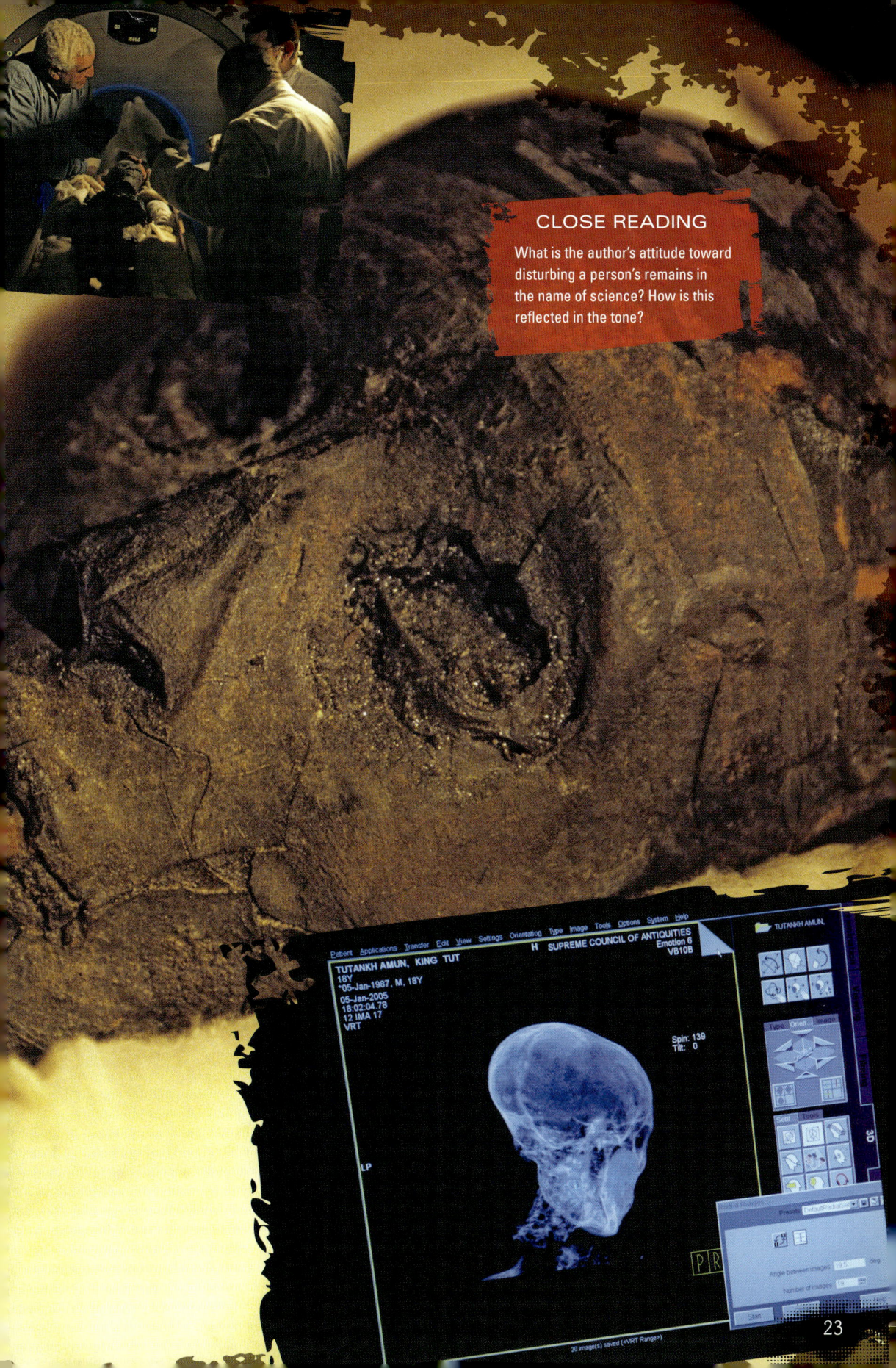

What is the author's attitude toward disturbing a person's remains in the name of science? How is this reflected in the tone?

Age Progressions

Age progression is another technology that forensic experts use to help identify a person. If a person has been missing for a long period of time, police will ask for an age progression to be produced. The age progression can give them a more accurate idea of what the person looks like now, helping them to narrow down their search and giving them a better chance at finding the missing person.

Age progressions were originally done by hand and are now done by computer. They involve taking an old image of the person and changing it to show what he probably looked like as he aged. Artists take into consideration variables such as lifestyle, occupation, nationality, and genetics, all of which help to determine how much weight the person might have gained as he aged, or how much hair he might have lost.

They can also add glasses, beards, mustaches, and updated hairstyles to create an educated guess about how the individual looks now.

Age progressions are often shown to the public in the hope that the missing person will be recognized and found. In some cases, missing children have been found as adults and finally reunited with their parents thanks to computerized age-progression technology.

> **FIRST READING**
> What variables do artists take into consideration when producing an age progression?

Aged 45

Aged 65

Aged 85

Building Faces: Lives Restored

When a skeleton is found, whether in a long-sealed tomb or buried in a garden behind a vacant house, we are left with many questions. The most important are: Who was this person, and how did he get here?

Sometimes, in the case of an ancient burial site, the answers are simple. In other cases, such as the discovery of Karen Price's bones, preliminary answers only lead to more questions. These questions can be answered by slow and detailed research that looks at many different factors, including health, lifestyle, occupation, and race. It is research that will help to rebuild not only faces but also identities, giving people back their rightful places in the world.

FIRST READING

According to the author, what are the most important questions one is left with when a skeleton is discovered?

...giving people back
their rightful
places in the world

CLOSE READING

How effective is the title of this section? How does it relate to the title of the book?

Think About the Text

Making Connections
Which of the following connections can you make to the information presented in *Building Faces*?

Text to Self

- Thinking about your own facial features and what defines your identity
- Considering the facial features of your family and friends and their unique characteristics
- Confirming personal values about human individuality and differences
- Taking a stance on issues of respect in investigatory work on human corpses
- Considering personal artifacts that define you in terms of age, gender, time, and location
- Forming opinions on the roles of anthropologists and forensic investigators and artists
- Thinking about how age might change your face

Text to Text/Media

Talk about other informational texts you may have read that have similar features. Compare the texts.

Text to World

Talk about situations in the world that connect to elements in the text.

Planning an Explanation

1. Select a topic that explains how something works or that gives reasons for some phenomena.

2. Brainstorm the ideas you want to focus on, featuring questions that ask *how* or *why* something happens.

Building Faces

- How do we identify what people from the past looked like?
- How do investigators create facial reconstructions?
- Why do we need to use forensic artists?
- How might facial and body features help with the identification of the dead?
- How does the human skeleton reveal information about age/gender/nationality/stature?
- How does 2-D, 3-D, and computerized imaging help to reconstruct faces for identification?
- How do artifacts help in the identification of people?
- How do we identify the remains of victims of crime?

3. Use multimedia resources for your investigation: Internet, library, journals, television documentaries, encyclopedias, newspapers, interviews with experts/organizations, DVDs, magazines, research documents . . .

4 Skim-read and take notes as you research. Record the references you used. Cross-reference your data.

Check out the credibility of the Web sites you used.
- Who composed the site, and are they experts?
- Does the information seem to be objective or based on opinion?
- Were there links from reputable sites to the site/s you used?

5 Sort through your notes, identifying key information and what is missing or what other information you need to know. Organize your information using headings/focus questions.

6 Make a plan.

Introduction
General background information that introduces the topic

⬇

Main ideas in a coherent and logical sequence.

| main idea | → | supporting details | → | supporting details | → | supporting details |

⬇

| main idea | → | supporting details | → | supporting details | → | supporting details |

⬇

| main idea | → | supporting details | → | supporting details | → | supporting details |

⬇

Conclusion
Statement encompassing an appropriate conclusion/summary

7 Think about visual interpretations that will elucidate and extend the information. You can use graphs, diagrams, charts, tables, cross-sections . . .

Writing an Explanation

Have you . . .
- stuck to relevant details/facts?
- focused on the main topic?
- explored causes and effects?
- used scientific and technical vocabulary?
- used the present tense? (Most explanations are written in the present tense.)
- written in a formal style that is concise and accurate?
- avoided unnecessary descriptive details, metaphors, or similes?
- avoided author bias or opinion?

Don't forget to revisit your writing. Do you need to change, add, or delete anything to improve your explanation?